Me Too!

Preschool Poetry

by CJ Heck

Barking Spiders Publishing
DuBois, PA

ISBN 0983932034
978-0-9839320-3-1

Poetry
Copyright 2011 C J Heck
All rights reserved
First Printing - 2011
Library of Congress #00-00000

Request for Information should be addressed to:

CJ Heck
705 W. Long Avenue
DuBois, PA 15801
814.249.1777
cjheck@barkingspiderspoetry.com

Other children's books by CJ Heck:
Barking Spiders (2000)
Barking Spiders 2 (2011)

Illustrations and Cover Design: CJ Heck
Credit given to Michelle Lenkner for illustration of child on front cover

Printed in USA 2011
Barking Spiders Publishing

This Book is lovingly dedicated to you,

my daughters, Carrie, Bethany and Heather.

You are everywhere within these pages,

as well as in my heart ...

I love you, girls

Acknowledgements

Grateful acknowledgement is made to the following, where some of these poems first appeared:

"Help, Monsters!", "Caterpillar", "Bumble Bee", in *Cambridge Express Student Book 1,* Cambridge University Press, India Pvt. Ltd.

"I Love Bugs", "Bedtime Prayer", *Art With Words, Poetry Quarterly,* Debra J. Harmes Kurth, Editor.

"To a Baby Firefly", in *Art With Words, Poetry Quarterly,* Debra J Harmes Kurth, Editor.

"Puddle Stompin'", "Naps", *Ultimate Guide to Celebrating Kids II,* Bluegrass Publishing.

Many thanks to the editors of the Bedford Journal Newspaper for entrusting this unknown writer many years ago with a children's column. You gave me the freedom to grow and spread my wings ... and I did.

Introduction

To my readers and friends:

Your enthusiasm for my first book, *Barking Spiders and Other Such Stuff,* has been heartwarming. This book is being published because of your desire for a book of poems just for preschoolers. It exists because of emails, letters, and conversations with parents, teachers, and my own grandchildren.

It is my sincere hope that *Me Too!* will also meet with your approval.

To all of you, I offer my warmest and most humble ... Thank You.

Hugs,
CJ

Table of Contents:

Bumble Bee

Today I watched a bumble bee.
He was on a pretty rose.
When I leaned in to look at him,
he stung me on my nose!

I wasn't going to squish him,
only watch and see ...
but I'll never get that close again
to a grouchy grumble bee.

Broccoli

Pipsy-dot-popsy
and diddly dot do
broccoli gags me.
Does it gag you?

It's icky, it's yucky,
a green pile I see,
and mommy keeps saying
it's so good for me.

I shouldn't be singing,
or making up rhymes.
I should be eating,
or be here a long time.

But broccoli smells
when it lays on my plate.
It's the stinkiest stuff,
the only veggie I hate.

I guess I could scoot it,
some here and some there,
then push it some more ...
ewww, it could fall on my chair

with little green piles of it
smushed on the floor!
(If they think I ate it,
they might give me more!)

But feathery freckles
and little blue beavers,
I just cannot eat it
and my dog, he won't either!

I told mommy and dad
I HATE broccoli.
I'll eat ANYthing else.
Yay! They gave me peas!

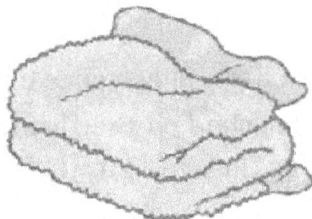

Blankies

Blankie was made to be slept with
Blankie was made to be hugged.
Blankie cares when mom and dad can't be there
'cause blankie was made to give love.

I sure do miss mine when it's in the wash,
(my blankie gets dirty, you see),
'cause EVERYWHERE I go, blankie goes, too,
with mommy and daddy and me.

Naps

I've tried to tell my mommy
I don't need a nap for me.
Naps are just for babies,
but we just don't agree.

I'm much too big to take one
and I've tried to tell her that,
but mom will never understand
why I don't want a nap.

So every day, I lay here,
with nothing else to do.
Sometimes, I even fall asleep
... and I think that she does, too!

Pretty Flower

I found a pretty flower,
food for bees and butterflies,
but when I gave it to my mom,
it put tears in mommy's eyes!

Why are mommies like that?
Pretty things can make them cry
just like a really sad thing.
Someday, will I know why?

Mommy said as I get older,
things won't all make sense,
but tears from pretty flowers
are always welcomed guests.

Scaredy Cat

I guess I'm just a scaredy cat.
I feel afraid of everything.
Sometimes I almost jump a mile
when I hear the telephone ring.

It's even scary in my room
so I have to have a light.
Who knows, there might be monsters
underneath my bed at night!

When daddy drives across a bridge,
I always hold my breath,
just in case the bridge falls down
so I won't be drowned to death.

Stick my hand inside a box?
First tell me what is in it.
Wait, my sister's yelling ...
I'll be back in just a minute.

I guess I'm braver than I thought!
Sissy made me sit beside her.
She said I was a HERO,
'cause I smushed a little spider.

My Lady Bug

Hi there, little lady bug.
Whatcha doing on my arm?
Please don't fly away.
I won't bring you any harm.

I'm glad to have you with me.
I was feeling all alone.
Somehow, I got me turned around.
I don't know my way back home.

I only took a *little* walk
behind a pretty butterfly,
but now I'm really scared and lost
and I think I'm going to cry.

Stay with me little lady bug.
Please don't fly away,
and when my mommy finds me,
come home with me and stay.

I'll let you share my bedroom
and when it's dark at night,
mommy leaves the lamp on
(monsters hate it when it's light).

Hey, that sounds like mommy!
It is! She's calling me!
Now you'll get to meet her.
You'll like her, wait and see.

Lady bug, why are you leaving?
I'll bet you're going home, too.
Thank you for being lost with me.
Bye lady bug, I love you!

9

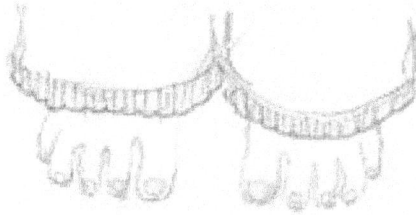

Ten Little Piggies

Ten little piggies
are standing in a line
and my mommy told me
the piggies are all mine.

One by one she points to them.
Every piggie has a name,
and then a place he goes to.
I really LOVE this game!

When mommy sings the song,
I see the piggies wiggle,
and when my mommy kisses them,
it makes me smile and giggle.

When the game is over,
we put them in warm socks.
Hmmm, just how many piggies
does a mom and daddy gots?

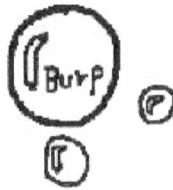

Belly Bubbles

My Daddy says a burp
is just a belly bubble.

Maybe so, I only know,
if it's LOUD, ya get in trouble!

Help! **Monsters!**

Help!
Monsters in my closet!
Monsters in the hall!
Monsters underneath my bed
and Monsters in the wall!

Monsters 'hind my bedroom door!
They're in the bathroom, too!
I know they're yucky green ones,
maybe even red or blue!

My bed feels like an island
with the Monsters everywhere ...
till mommy says goodnight to them.
Then they all just disappear.

Mud Pies

Today I'm cooking the dinner.
I use a spoon made of wood.
I know just how to cook it
so EVERYthing I make tastes good.

I made meatloaf, but not any onions,
and veggies without any beans.
See how I squish the smashed 'tatoes
beside the burgers and cheese?

Next I will make ice cream salad.
Cooking dinner is really fun work!
Here's shovels and buckets of jello
and marshmallow pies for dessert.

Uh oh ... now it's raining.
Mommy will bring me inside.
Rain sure is wrecking my cooking,
but it will make MORE mud outside!

Puddle Stompin'

I like saying "spring has sprung"
'cause I like the way it sounds,
and spring brings with it lots of rain,
(God's wringing out His clouds).

Yay! Rain means puddle stompin'.
After rain, they're EVERYwhere.
No shoes or socks, I'm barefoot!
I get wet, but I don't care.

I don't think my mommy likes it
'cause I get muddy ... ewww,
but puddles just can't help it.
Somehow mud gets in there, too!

Uh oh, here comes mommy.
Hey, look at mommy run!
Mommy's puddle stompin' too?
NOW it's REALLY fun!

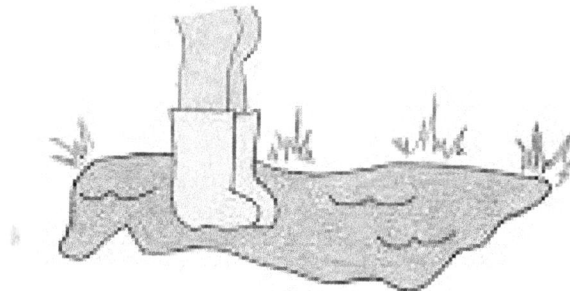

Breakfast Child

Early this morning, I spilled my milk.
It dripped on the kitchen floor
and when I tried to wipe it up,
I slipped and spilled some more.

Then the cereal box tumbled down
and Cheerios went everywhere.
Little O's in the milk on the floor!
Little O's stuck in my hair!

Oh my, I thought, I made a mess!
Dad and mommy will be mad ...
Oops! I slipped and fell in it, too!
Then I felt really bad.

Then mommy and daddy came in.
They were laughing at my mess!
They said I looked really funny
sitting in my own breakfast.

Angels All Around Me

Angels all around me.
Angels high above.
Pretty angels everywhere
guarding me with love.

Angels by my bed
help me start my prayers,
while other angels hurry
mom and daddy up the stairs.

When it's time to say night-night,
my angels' jobs aren't through.
When I close my eyes to sleep,
they watch me all night, too.

Angels all around me.
Angels high above.
Pretty angels everywhere
guarding me with love.

Now I'm Three and I Know ...

I know *never* touch fire, that's HOT,
but I can touch ice, 'cause it's not,
and puppies are soft and kitties are, too,
so's most of the stuff moms and dads give to you.

I know NEVER tell people they're fat
'cause it will hurt them if I do that,
and rocks aren't for throwing at others
but it's okay to throw pillows at brothers.

I know daddy says swears I can't say
and I have to wear clothes out to play ...
'cuz one time I went outside naked & Mrs. Johnson saw me & she called
mommy & mommy came outside & got mad *(sniff)* & she yelled at me
(sniffle) & I had to sit in a chair for a whole time out *(sniff)* and ...

I know cookies smell better than cheese
and to get one, I have to say "please",
and how to go pee in the potty
but not in my pants, 'cause that's naughty.

I know flowers don't need any feet
and no dessert if I don't eat my meat
and I got to blow boogers in tissue
and don't wipe off where ladies kiss you.

When I wake mommy up, *never* holler
and pennies aren't more than a dollar
and scissors are NEVER for cutting my hair,
the barber does that, (but I hate going there).

I laugh 'cause it's better than cry
and you can't squeeze a worm, it will die,
and daddy will laugh if I'm burping
and mommy's kiss helps what is hurting.

I know SO many things, now I'm three
and this stuff helps ME be a good ME.
I know lots more than I did when I'm two
of the stuff I can do and I can't do.

Playhouse

Mommy, come inside our playhouse!
Me and Sissy worked all day.
We made a door and window.
Come on in and you can play.

Me and Sissy can scoot over
so you'll have a place to sit.
Thanks for bringing pans and spoons
so we can work on it.

Over here we made a kitchen,
over there, a living room.
We never have to clean it.
We don't even need a broom!

We didn't make a bedroom,
so no beds we have to make.
Uh oh, Sissy, look outside!
See the big snowflakes?

I guess that it will be okay.
Our whole house is made of snow.
We scooped it from a snowdrift
and now our house will grow!

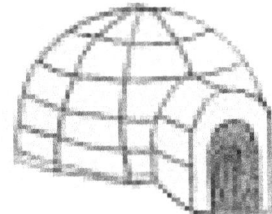

I Love Bugs

I love teeny tiny ants
and itchy bitsy fleas,
spiders, big and little,
and grouchy grumble bees,

butterflies that flutter by,
and beetles when they run
from marching caterpillars.
I think bugs are fun!

Skeeters like to bite me,
but fireflies, they don't,
and flies that get inside the house
could bite, but they won't.

Silly racing centipedes
and slow and slimy slugs
are my *very* special favorites.
I   love   bugs!

Me, Myself, and I

Daddy calls me diddle-dog.
Papa calls me chief.
I'm always baby brother
to my sister -- oh good grief!

Nana calls me punkin'.
Mama calls me little man.
I'm boo-boo bear to grammy
... gee, I wonder who I am.

I guess it's like my sneakers.
Some call them tennis shoes.
Both names mean the same thing.
It doesn't matter which I use.

Or maybe, like my puppy.
Some people call them hounds.
It doesn't really matter,
'cause they both make barking sounds.

You know, it's really not so bad
they don't all call me the same.
I feel kinda-sorta special
that I have so many names!

Nuffing on My Plate

I'm sad. I don't like nuffing
that's laying on my plate.
Maybe it will go away
if I just sit and wait.

I sure don't like the liver
and I never, EVER could.
Can I have peanut butter
with grape jelly? THAT is good!

The smashed potatoes are okay,
yucky gravy, it is NOT.
It's like having icky oatmeal
and I hate that stuff a lot.

I *almost* like the green beans.
they're green, just like my frog,
but NO ONE likes dumb broccoli,
not even Hank, my dog!

Uh oh, mommy says we're having
chocolate pudding for a treat ...
maybe if I hold my nose
stuff won't taste bad to me.

Uh Oh ...

Uh oh. When mommy's on her knees
in front of me, it's clear,
there's something she wants to say
that I won't want to hear.

(thinking) ... Did I hit my sister?
Did I maybe tell a lie?
Did I forget to pick up toys?
This time, I don't know why.

At least she doesn't stand and yell
the way some mommys do,
or scream right in my face
to tell me what to do.

Did I spill my glass of milk?
Was I naughty at my school?
Did I forget to clean a mess?
Did I maybe break a rule?

Sometimes I know what I did wrong
and I tell her there and then.
It helps to say I'm sorry
and I won't do that again.

Now I just don't understand
what I might have done.
Hey! I just got a hug and kiss!
This time, it was for FUN!

My blood was almost gone!
Well, that's not *exactly* true ...
but still, it really scared me
and it woulda scared you, too.

Daddy always told me,
"Don't pet dogs that you don't know.
All dogs aren't like our Frankie.
If you don't know them, let them go."

But this dog was really nice.
Well, that's not *exactly* true ...
he *pretended* that he liked me,
but he growled some at me, too.

I think I shoulda let him go,
just like daddy said to do.
Then I *never* woulda hadda go
to the EEE ARR to get glued.

The EEE ARR

Oooo, today I got some stitches.
Well, that's not *exactly* true ...
but glue's kinda-sorta like them.
Glue holds skin together, too.

Mommy took me to the EEE ARR
'cause my blood was everywhere!
It was on my shirt and pants.
See? It's still right here, and there!

Caterpillar

Fuzzy caterpillar
with your million-jillion feet,
how do you know which foot should go
when you're walking on that leaf?

You make it look so easy,
right-left-right, the way you do.
Sometimes, MY feet get tangled up
and I have only TWO ...

Mr. 'Tato Head

I am really very angry
and I am very really mad.
I can't find my happy face,
it's gone, and now I'm sad.

I was playing with a toy
called Mr. 'Tato Head
and my big brother yelled at me.
I don't like the thing he said.

I was sticking in two eyes,
then I found a 'just right' nose,
but when I stuck his mouth in,
that wasn't where it goes.

So, I pulled the mouth back out
and I stuck it back in ... there.
But when I tried to give him ears,
his mouth fell on my chair!

I pushed the mouth in one more time,
then I poked in both his shoes.
(I couldn't find his purple hat,
but that's what I ALWAYS lose).

Then the whole thing fell apart!
EVERYthing came all unhooked!
That's when my brother yelled at me.
"Silly, you don't use a 'tato that's
COOKED!"

To a Baby Firefly ...

Little baby firefly,
when your night is through,
does your mommy tuck you in
and tell you she loves you?

Does she kiss your forehead
and say as she hugs you tight,
"Day-day little sleepyhead,
close your eyes, blink out your light."

My Snowman

Snow was flaking all around
then gently piling on the ground.

Just tiny puffs when floating free,
but stuck together, I could see

it's like a voice that's singing for us,
or a lot, like in a chorus.

I rolled some up and stacked it high
and made a happy snowman guy.

I'm glad it's that way just with snow
and that's not how we children grow,

'cause on a warm and sunny day,
my snowman slowly melts away.

As he melts, he gets so thin ...
I wish, like me, that he had skin.

Muddles

Splashing-sploshing mud in puddles.
I will name what I made, "muddles".
Run and jump, my feet go splishy,
bare toes feel good, squashy-squishy.

Uh oh, muddles freckled my new pants!
I wiped it worse, 'cause it's on my hands!
Dripsy-dropsy EVERYplace!
It's in my hair! It's on my face!

It's on my shirt, and there, and THERE!
Muddles got me EVERYwhere!
Muddles bubbles in my smell,
is it in BOTH nose holes?   I can't tell,

and every twirl I go, it goes,
and here comes mommy with the hose.
Mommy said just look at me ...
I can't, 'cause muddles got in my see.

but there aren't muddles in my ears
and mommy's yells fill up my hears.
Now dripples are raining down, oh well,
it's raining muddles off my smell.

My poor muddles, now they're moosh.
I slippered and sat right in the goosh.
Hose raining muddles off my thumb,
and raining muddles from on my bum,

now there's NOwhere muddles stayed
'cause the dripples made it go away.
I can't play now, not here, OR there,
'cause I'm in a corner on a chair

and mommy's washing all my clothes.
She said, "Why muddles? I don't know!"
Would I still have so many troubles
if I named it somethin' else, NOT
muddles?

The Swinging Song

Bye Oh Bye up,
Bye Oh Bye down,
Bye Oh Bye feet
way off the ground.

Swing-ing, swing-ing,
I love swing-ing.

Bye Oh Bye high,
Bye Oh Bye low,
Bye Oh Bye faster,
look at me go.

Swing-ing, swing-ing,
I love swing-ing.

Bye Oh Bye flying
up to the sky.
Bye Oh Bye push me
higher than high.

Swing-ing, swing-ing,
I love swing-ing.

Bye Oh Bye eyes
are closing now.
Bye Oh Bye head
is nodding down.

Swing-ing, swing-ing,
I love swing-ing.

Bye Oh Bye gently
Bye Oh Bye slow.
Bye Oh Bye *shhhhhh ...*
to sleep I go.

Swing-ing, swing-ing,
I love swing-ing.

Bedtime Prayer

Now I lay me
down in bed.

All my prayers
and night-nights said.

Snuggle bunny, teddy bear,
toasty blankie, all are here.

Out with the light
so dreams will come.

Thank you, God.
Now, where's my thumb?

(Night-Night)

Bye Bye

About the Author:

A native of Ohio, CJ Heck currently lives in Du Bois Pennsylvania. She is a published poet, writer, blogger, and children's author, who loves writing fiction and nonfiction short stories, memoirs and personal essays. She is also a Vietnam War widow.

For more information about CJ, or to invite her to your school or organization, please visit her website or call 814-249-1777.

Barking Spiders Poetry for Children:
www.barkingspiderspoetry.com

www.ingramcontent.com/pod-product-compliance
Lightning Source LLC
Chambersburg PA
CBHW080938040426
42443CB00015B/3469